Bingo in the House of Babel

a play by Stan's Cafe

ISBN 978-1-913185-12-1

Published by Stan's Cafe
Birmingham, UK
2020

www.stanscafe.co.uk

Bingo in the House of Babel © Stan's Cafe 1994
Photos © James Yarker 1994
Publication © Stan's Cafe 2020

Contents:

Bingo in the House of Babel	1
Bonus Material	
Original programme notes	24
An interview for Nuffield Theatre, Lancaster	25
The making of *Bingo In The House Of Babel* and the slow remaking of Stan's Cafe	29
99 numbers for finding lost people	33

Bingo in the House of Babel

The Setting

The House of Babel is a vast tower of libraries stacked on top of each other. Each library holds the thoughts of one great thinker, an analogue artificial intelligence which allows researchers to ask the long dead thinker any question they wish. Given all the variables involved getting an answer from the library requires considerable skill, which is why so many librarians are employed.

Bingo in the House of Babel is set in the library of Einstein's brain. Although it is a much consulted library, the room dedicated to volumes answering the question if the great man would like a cup of tea or coffee is something of a backwater. The librarians have spare time, time to think, time to worry about their own existence and about the rumour that, for reasons of economy, some of their number may be robots. What if this were them and they didn't know? Maybe that would explain why they feel like this.

Nothing has been the same since the fire.

The Script

This was a devised piece in which images, choreography and music were considered as important as the words. The actors' original scripts were these words with a few stage directions. For this version of the script those stage directions have been elaborated upon in order to give readers a greater sense of the full show.

An old fashioned bingo machine comes to life in a burnt out library.

Amanda, in skirt suit, spins under a down light, a cardboard box over her eyes (virtual reality goggles).

Black out.

Amanda stands downstage looking out dizzy and frightened.

Floor-boards rattle in two different areas of the stage.

Two librarians break through the floor and sit up. They smile at each other then see Amanda.

Ray remains in his hole, Sarah climbs out of her hole and walks very slowly toward Amanda, eventually she holds her hand.

Amanda, surprised, turns and looks Sarah up and down. They smile at each other and still holding hands face the audience.

Sarah shows Amanda an exercise, holding your hand flat and in turn separating each finger from its right hand neighbour and not the left. Ray can do this, Amanda cannot.

Sarah is now wary of Amanda but is won back with the childish joke of creating a toilet with one curled hand and it's lid with the other flat over the top. The women play 'cleaning the toilet' with Amanda lifting the lid and circling a finger in the bowl, they squeal with laughter.

Ray, confused, replicates the gag, he can't see how it is funny. Emerging from his hole he shows Amanda a reflex action, hitting the inside of his elbow to make his hand flick up. They find this highly amusing. Sarah cannot replicate the action.

As if to cover this embarrassment or to introduce herself Amanda repeats the library slogan.

Amanda:	I believe in stories and the power of fiction.
	I believe in the word being flesh,
	Books as our lives and our graves,
	This room as Einstein...
Ray}	Freud.
Sarah}	Stalin.
Amanda:	...Einstein living on beyond time.
	The library is our history and future...
Ray:	*[Slightly mocking]*
	its maintenance my duty, my dream and my joy.
	The truth is the false made physical.
	I believe in invention and lies.
	Real is a special pretend.
Amanda:	*[The others join in]*
	I believe in stories and the power of fiction.
	I believe in the word being flesh,
All:	Books as our lives and our graves.
	This room as Einstein living on beyond time.

                The library is our history and future,
                Its maintenance my duty, my dream and my joy.
                The truth is the false made physical.
                I believe in invention and lies.
                Real is a special pretend.
Ray: This slow time.
                This eel time.
                This distant, relative, drug time.
[The others look at him slightly scared and back off]

[Black out]

Nowhere.

Ray spins in silhouette, books fly all around him scattering ash and torn pages. An unbearable noise assaults the ears. Slowly the light and sound ease to reveal the library and a playful scene of Ray staggering around being pelted by books excavated from holes in the floor by Amanda and Sarah.

There are improvised protestations to stop the throwing. Ray gathers books and checks their spines. The throwing now is sporadic, revealing frustrations. A book bound by an elastic band is found by Ray, inside there is a sandwich, he sits to eat it whilst reading, as he finishes a page he tears it out, screws it up and throws it away.

Sarah takes a pair of cereal box VR goggles from under the stage, Amanda agrees to put on her's as well.

With their goggles on, the women explore their virtual environments and the objects they contain. The objects they encounter in their physical world are reinterpreted by their goggles. The women are in different virtual worlds but occasionally the improvised text or physical relationship suggests that they could be in the same scene.

Amanda is in Star Trek testing dust from the floor, using a tissue and an ink pad as props.

Amanda: Mmm interesting. This is a strange planet. Just as I'd thought, It's alive. I, I'm so hot, I, Scotty, Scotty, where are you...oh my God, it's the ship, they've shrunk the ship, don't worry men, I'll, ahhh the noise.

Sarah plays the part of a French sex worker and then a hair dresser with a ball of string.

Sarah: Why don't you come inside? My you're sweating. Why don't you take your jacket off and lay down here beside me. Oh dear, you've got some nasty knots in here, what kind of conditioner have you been using. Oh dear well tell you what I can do. I'll take out the split ends at the bottom and taper it through the front but you're going to have to take more care of it yourself.

Amanda is on her death bed giving a relative a valuable stapler when she is mistaken by Sarah for a water bed. Amanda in turn mistakes Sarah for an alien. Sarah is then concerned that in her excitement she has punctured the bed, for an alien. Sarah takes photos with a hole punch and crosses the stage with a lamp shade megaphone, Amanda walks in the country stepping on a particularly smelly book and feeding a chair a crunched up sheet of paper.

Sarah's box develops a fault sending her on a bad trip clutching an old floor board, Amanda is Mae West apparently telling Sarah she can't come crawling back to win her affections with cheap jewellery. Both boxes become faulty Amanda snatches her's off in time but it is left to Ray to disarm Sarah who is frantically trying to keep the monster away by flailing around with the plank.

Ray is powerless to stop Sarah thinking she's been shot, she falls to the ground thrashing around in hysteria. Ray eventually grows desperate and tries to heal her, pinning her to the ground.

Ray: You're not going to die
You're not going to die
You're not going to die

It's stopping it's stopping
The bleeding's stopping
I can see it
It's stopping, hold on
Hold on, you're not going to die
The bleeding stopping
There's the bullet
It's rising up, the bullet's coming out
It's a miracle, it's a miracle.

The bleeding's stopping and the bullet's rising up and you're not going to die. You're not going to die. There's the bullet and the bleeding's stopped and you're healing. The skin's coming together, you're healing. It's coming together, you're healing. There's a scab forming and it's drying and it's dried, now it's fallen off and there's not even going to be a scar.

That's it, you're healed.

Sarah has calmed down and been convinced of the healing but is still anxious. Ray tries to reassure her but only succeeds when he produces a chair for her.

Ray: Hide behind this, it's impenetrable.

A tender phone call ensues via a pair of scissors as Sarah's phone and Ray's improvised reassuring responses as her mother sending her father to pick her up.

This scene cross fades with Amanda downstage starting a monologue.

Amanda: Numbers 1 to 29 are The Unpalatable Truths, Secret Memories and The Blessings Of Incompetence.

When I first came here I thought it was going to be really exciting. "Einstein's Mind!" I thought , "It's not very romantic but there are few more important minds in the library," I thought.

I was excited at going to work in the central tower, "That's where all the great librarians are supposed to work," I thought, "maybe I'll meet them in the lift" but I never did and when I arrived they didn't know what to do with me and before I knew it, there I was stuck in the 'Tea or Coffee? Room' of Einstein's mind, where no one ever comes and when they do it's only to wind you up, because no one really wants to know what he wants to drink any more.

"Would Mr. Einstein like a cup of tea or a cup of coffee?" they ask and look at you like you're a nobody. "That depends," I say. "On what?" they say. "On lots of things," I say. Then I ask "what date is it?" and they never know and have to make it up, when I say I can't help without it. Then I ask what kind of tea or coffee they're offering, because it makes a big difference to Einstein what kind of coffee he's being offered. Although he generally doesn't like tea so much, there are many occasions when he will have it, especially if it's at a friend's house in the afternoon on a hot Sunday.

The coffee's got a hundred different shelves for all the different types and the tea's a smaller section but much more complex. So, if you're not sure what's on offer you can spend the whole day walking backwards and forwards between them

> all, backwards and forwards and backwards and forwards and you never get anywhere.
>
> And sometimes the people get angry and shout "This is stupid, you don't know do you?" and I shout right back at them "Of course we know, we can answer any tea or coffee question for Einstein, it's just going to take some time, all right!" Then, if I'm in the mood, I say "Ask him if he wants a tea or coffee why don't you? He can't even drink it, but you don't ask me and I can and I will, thank you very much for asking, I'll have a coffee, black with two sugars".

Ray approaches to hold her hand in a reprise of an earlier motif, he is interrupted by the final bit of text.

> I often think "Why don't they get a machine to do this? Why don't we even have a computer with the answers to help us? Some parts of the library do". I think "Those librarians must have an easy life".

Ray starts telling his story to Amanda but soon turns it out to the audience.

Ray: Numbers 30 to 59 are Body Proof, Instructions For Self Revelation and Things They Call Love.

> When I started here I thought that the library would be a friendly place, I thought I would have loads of spare time to look up interesting facts and learn things, I thought that I would be able to leave here and that when I did I would be a better and wiser man, but it's not true nothing they tell you is true.
>
> I've been here years now, years and years and there's no chance of leaving, because it's taken

me all this time just to become an assistant librarian, which just means I work harder than a full librarian and that I'm just stuck in this one room all of the time, with the others always talking about me and testing me and asking all sorts of trick questions and some times I look at them and think how sad they all look and I feel sorry for them, not knowing what it's like outside and sometimes I just wish I was back pushing the trolley.

They said I would learn things here, but it's all just messed up and useless. All the best books were lost years and years before any of us were born and the old librarians used to tell you stories but most of the time it was just rubbish, things that weren't real memories, just old dreams and photographs and legends. Sometimes the things they remembered came straight from boxes and they'd happened to me as well. And before I gave up listening to their rubbish, they told me about the lost rooms in the heart of the library, were all the best books were, with all the best titles:

The Book Of Alternative Nows, A Directory Of Hearts Never Broken, What You Thought Yesterday, What You Will Think Tomorrow And Why You Think What You're Thinking As You Read This Book, Book of Auto Suggestions, Reading Other People's Minds By Phone, The Lives Of Those Who Might Have Lived, A Book For Dying Young, The Book Of Forgetting and *99 Numbers For Finding Lost People.*

An embarrassed pause.

> I've got a secret. When I first arrived at the library, I had a job as a trolley-boy and the section

head called me into his office and said "Morning boy". "Good morning Sir," I said. And I remember his office, it was like a stationery cupboard with an oak desk jammed in it. And I remember thinking he must have to climb over the desk to get to that chair and imagining his fat arse in the air and nearly laughing.

"Boy, do you know what's in this library?" He asked "Yes Sir, books Sir" I said, then he threw a hole punch at me. "Not books boy, people, all the great people and you know what you show in front of great people?" He was holding a paperweight and I was bleeding from the hole punch wound, so didn't say anything. "RESPECT" he bellowed, "So do what you're told and keep out of trouble. I don't want to see you again until you're an assistant librarian, understand?".

This is the scar from the hole punch.

Sarah: Once I got into the top secret area. It was years ago, late at night after the Christmas party. I wandered round for ages scaring myself, trying door handles at random. I was lost and drunk and found myself in the Day Dream Room. All Einstein's real and potential day dreams were filed neatly away in glass cabinets. I skimmed along the shelves and picked

Sarah & R: a book at random, it was a catalogue for

Ray: *Idle Speculation On The Shape Of Clouds In Blue Summer Skies.* I flicked through the book, thinking, "why books in our section always smell of

Ray & A: sick

Sarah:	and this one smells of cut grass". I skimmed through the catalogue index and found a page of references for Headmaster Clouds Chased Across The Sky By
Sarah & R:	Dog Clouds.
Amanda:	Without thinking I took out my pen and wrote "RESPECT, fat arse" at the bottom of the page. Then I put the book back on the shelf. I bet it's still there today, just like my hole punch scar.
All:	This is my secret.

There is a reprise of the opening, each character in turn is reminded of the exercise they couldn't do, finger separation, arm reflex and finally Ray is confronted by two toilets, lids raised. Black out.

Nowhere. Violent music and bleak cross light, Sarah clutches a pile of books to her chest, Gavin walks slowly towards her and holds her hand, both wear cardboard boxes. Crossfade to Amanda picking up bingo balls, inventing stupid little calls to go with the numbers before dropping them down the shoot. The others join in. When there are none left they call Bingo. Nothing happens. Bathos. Black out.

Dim lighting, they clear a space centre stage and stand back.

Sarah:	*[Tentatively]* Albert, if there is pain here, let it be written not felt. Albert, if there is confusion let it be beautiful mystery. If this is the face of infinity let it be mine. Albert, if this is the end let it also be mine
Amanda:	and let it be soon.

Sarah puts on her box and is slowly led forward. A curious seance is enacted to conjure up the fire and its memories.

Ray: In this decay time of strangeness. When so many robots walk the land with such calm.
In this time, this curious, dubious half time, only ninety nine numbers remain.
Ninety nine numbers for finding lost people

Amanda: This is a slow time, a fall time, a night time. This is the zone where minds are leaking from their books.
The corridors are haunted by the half realised thoughts of the dead.

Ray: As you walk through that zone you pass through a thousand emotions, none of them your own.

Amanda: This is where you gain knowledge simply by breathing.

Ray: We said, "these are dark corridors full of fighting that we shouldn't ever walk down. These are dark corridors of dank intrigue where we should never walk".

Amanda: "These are the dripping tunnels of things we should never think".

Ray: This is the dead-end library of no answers.

Amanda: The library is diseased, ticking, slowly rotting down.
This library is running out of thoughts.
This library is exhausted, dried, dying, ready to be burnt.

Ray: You plug yourself into the wall of a long lost person's brain and hear them think of you.

Ray & A: "You are my disease".

Ray: And the last time I saw you, all those years ago I think I remember saying "I'll look you up next time I pass this way". I've passed this way. I've never looked you up.

Sarah: I said "Put me down Johnny. For God's sakes, put me down. Don't play these games with me"

Amanda: You think you hear inside your head as books are taken from the wall. The dust dirt books of solid thought in simple code.
All codes to keep you from yourself are simple, or so you think.

Ray: She knows the language of fire.

Sarah: "Rip the pages Johnny, cure them for me".

Ray: It's time to turn from here before it all blows.

Sarah: I can feel it Johnny, feel it on my face. That's a breeze Johnny. Can you ever remember feeling a breeze in here? One that wasn't the closing of a book? That's the breath of God, Johnny.

Amanda: She said "That's the breath of God, come to blow away all this confusion".

Ray: Maybe you smell petrol...

Amanda: maybe you fake a laugh...

Ray: maybe you mutter...

Sarah: "Never thought so much of nothing. Never thought so much of nothing much".

Ray: Maybe you smell petrol, maybe you smell sulphur cutting through the mildew stench of curling

	minds. Maybe you climbed the shelves to find the noxious fumes.
Amanda:	Maybe you smelt petrol and wished it was in your blood.
Sarah:	Stalin thought "Who is this spectre troubling my mind with its disorder?" Joseph screamed at nights "who will cleanse me of this ghost?" There's fear coming off these books, I recognise its smell.
Ray:	So torch her Johnny, now you're inside torch her spines and blur her mind with incense smoke.
Sarah:	Torch her Johnny...
Ray:	torch the fucking lot of her.
Sarah:	It's catching Johnny, it's burning and there's nothing I can do. Johnny don't let this happen. What am I supposed to do? I can feel it now Johnny, I can feel it on my face and it's getting hotter. It's raining down. It's raining fucking fire Johnny. What the hell! That's no blizzard, that's paper!
Amanda:	We shouted. "Look out Johnny, the library's throwing its guts at us!"
Ray:	Books are hitting the walls all around us and we're up to our knees in other people's fears and still it keeps on coming.
Amanda:	And momentarily full of joy we cried
All:	"Last one out's a pile of old scrap!"

Ray: And there are flashing blues and yellows, violent aching arcs of colour scorching everything in sight and the floor is shaking and books are falling from the walls. The compulsion is growing strong.

Sarah: "Don't listen, don't listen".

Amanda: Don't let yourself hear.

Ray: You're screaming aloud and a louder still as the sense is flooding off the page.

Sarah: "I've seen all this before, show me something new, show me something I've never known before"...

Amanda: you say. And with an old Bic pen gouging out an altered legend in the margin...

Sarah & A: "Don't believe a word of it!"

Sarah: "I hate and renounce myself as a coward!"

Amanda: You hear the library virus "I hate and fucking kill myself for ever!"

Sarah: "I shall touch no being".

Ray: You are closing in on these French corners, these confused corridors where entropy serves to level order on the random, fearful, raging, nihilchaos.

Amanda: Burn yourself into yourself. You're burnt now and doors that never seem to close and numbers called from every corner.

Ray: Like, 91.

Amanda: "Getting home alive".

Ray:	92.
Amanda:	"Kicking out for fear of laying down".
Ray:	93.
Amanda:	"Hiding in mirrors".
Ray:	94.
Amanda:	"Falling away from everything for ever". "Saying no to every question ever asked". "Hating everyone at all times for ever". There's no where, no hope, no lasting thought of anything at all. "I'll take a tea and kill myself for ever. I'll hole myself up in here and cut out all the parts that feel pain. There are no people in these corridors. There are no people in these corridors. There are no people who think of you, who think these thoughts as you do. You're on your fucking own now Johnny, don't say I didn't warn you.
Ray:	There is a book in here, the fire-proof book, a proof against water and voodoo and lies and deceit, The Indestructible book.
Sarah:	I know the language of fire. "I've lost control in here, you've burnt out some vital part of me" it's Sylvia.
Ray:	You shuffled along the wall guarding the remains of her room. "They've installed an impossible pattern in my mind. There is no hope or chance to stay like that".
Amanda:	"I hate and renounce as a coward every sensation and every being".
Sarah:	I can smell burning, hear the squealing of texts.

> I can feel heat on my face, the charring of hopes.
> Salome's thoughts are "cut out your own heart under local anaesthetic".
> And as Joseph K thought to himself on the corridors of nothing "one hundred, two hundred, three hundred, counting".

Smoke pours from between the floorboards and red light flares. Amanda nails herself under the floor, Ray and Sarah gather piles of books and throw them into the inferno. Ray chalks Proof Against Fire across his clothes and leaves a torn paper trail as the bingo machine is approached. Amanda emerges from the floor clutching a book whose two pages read "Yes" and "No".

Books are nailed to posts. The bingo machine is pushed around the set. Music eases to emotive piano. The fire dies down.

Ray has two box-files and is sitting on a chair. The women whisper fragments from the torn paper that litters the stage, they pass the best to Ray who whispers them as well.

Sarah: *[As other monologues]* into at all I I things and out down some something some with was sleep cards sort fire of the and that the leaving bingo my hand my I library I numbers I like hoped couldn't it away rather it its enjoying couldn't cracking added play burnt when with was never was how was sleep troubles extra had bingo sleep book blood bingo been because of do words code random solve library numbers found sleep nights I I a I that I me I out in me my and my the the the the all than at that to with code and message in when and coffee and and play burnt from to like but automatic easy about all from to filled all marking library worries learnt have in in I'd there off numbers until bingo looked found carried about codes times once manage subconscious understand thought from all did had come some this had there anywhere yourself its talk to get things couldn't was come these had and.

Numbers 60 to 99 Jokes, Keys To A Robot Existence, Instincts of Almost Animals, The Impossible Numbers.

Ray is throwing a blizzard of paper scraps over Amanda who is spinning round and trying to catch them, she falls and the paper continues to fall lit from either side red and orange.

Amanda: Einstein thought "who'll wash my socks now and who'll make me tea and, should I want it, coffee for today?"

Ray: There were corridors where thoughts of lust flushed the ceilings red and burned a heat of immanent fire through the walls. "Tonight Louis tonight of all nights, tonight" this is my thought, you think, as you think on for miles, why have I come all this way to find just my own thoughts again?

Sarah: And you read aloud to us all, while we were sleeping, the thoughts of Chairman Mao. "King Kong Fooey" you said and we all laughed in our sleep because we realised you were making it all up and never meant what it was you said.

Amanda: Somewhere in all this there lies a robot.
If it's me, please never let me know.

Ray: "I need more space than this," he thought to himself as he continued to type, "I need more space and someone to read".

Amanda: I know the language of fire.
And Gertrude Stein thought "who'll wash my socks if Alice doesn't and who'll make my tea or should I want it, coffee?"

Ray: And I say in these words that no one can hear...

Ray & S: "Why is it that I am standing here alone?"

Amanda: And when everything had stopped and it was just me and me, then I said to my-selves in the quietest whisper ever

Sarah & A: "They'll never look for us here".

Ray: It's so empty in here, no thoughts to help me home. I'm broken down. There are no thoughts for me in here. I'm on my own. There is nowhere else. I'm locked in here.

Sarah: And if there are coffee thoughts, let them be black, unsweetened and unstirred.

Mixed: And if its Wednesday and if it's nineteen forty five and if its over an hour since the last cup and if the humidity is high and the pollen count is low and if there is no smell then, cross referencing as a substitute for thinking gives us a reading of a mind and, hold on, it's coming now and if there has previously been no history of horrific coffee at this place and if there has been hard thinking done and arrogance to be shown then all things point to... coffee.

Ray: But don't take our word, there are many, many

more things we have to ask before we can be sure.

The bingo machine comes to life throwing up balls, a performer calls these numbers and a voice from the speakers reads the phrase that goes with them. If the number corresponds to one of the ten each performer has memorised they answer 'yes' and chalk their number on one of the ten planks of the back wall. The game continues until someone has won. Not all balls need be put in the machine but beyond this the game must not be cheated. Winning the game ends the show with a shout of "House!"

Original Programme Notes

Bingo in the House of Babel
by
Stan's Cafe

*In this decay time of strangeness,
when so many robots walk the land with such calm,
In this time, this curious, dubious, half-time,
only ninety nine numbers remain,
ninety nine numbers for finding lost people.*

Devised and Performed by
Sarah Dawson, Amanda Hadingue, Ray Newe

Direction & text	James Yarker
Voice	Graeme Rose
Music	Richard Chew
with	Jon Ward
Lighting & operation	Paul Arvidson
Set	Stan's Cafe
with	Lucy Freeman
Publicity design	Simon Ford
Photography	Stan's Cafe

Special thanks to: Peter Fletcher
Tom Miles at BBC Sound Archives and mac

Commissioned by mac, Birmingham
and funded by the Arts Council of Great Britain,
West Midlands Arts and Birmingham City Council.
Stan's Cafe is a member of the Independent Theatre Council

Stan's Cafe hope to make a poetic theatre of ideas. A form of theatre in which audiences are given the materials and space to build their own stories. Just as there are many questions embedded in each piece, so there is no single answer to search for.

An Interview For Nuffield Theatre Lancaster

Who are the members of Stan's Cafe?
The personnel of Stan's Cafe (pronounced Caff) change with each piece of work. Based round a core membership of James Yarker and Graeme Rose the company is a loose collective of young artists from a number of disciplines.

For *Bingo in the House of Babel* other members are: Deviser/performers: Sarah Dawson, Amanda Hadingue and Ray Newe. Composer: Richard Chew (long time collaborator) and technician: Paul Arvidson

Which of you are Lancaster Graduates?
Both James (1990) and Graeme (1987) are Lancaster graduates as are Amanda (1988), Ray (1989), Paul (1991) and our graphic designer Simon Ford (1990).

What degree subjects did you read?
We are all basically Theatre Studies graduates though there is some English and Independent Studies thrown in there along with Simon's Visual Arts Degree.

Graeme stuck around in Lancaster to form glory what glory theatre co-operative, which was how I met him. Amanda is a superb actress and started getting work immediately on graduating and moved to London. Ray got his equity card shortly after graduating appearing in a pantomime at The Duke's in Lancaster, he moved to Manchester and from there to Drama School in London. Paul now runs his own theatre lighting business from Lancaster.

How did you form Stan's Cafe?
After graduating I made Super 8 films, wrote scripts and did terrible jobs for a year. It slowly dawned on me that I was missing presenting my work to an audience and working with other people in a collaborative context, so I decided I had to form a company. Fortunately at just this time Graeme's old company was breaking up. We respected each others work,

knew we had similar ambitions and got on well, so whilst sitting in Stan's Cafe decided to form a company. The most difficult thing was deciding on a name.

How did you cope financially at the outset?
As all companies do, we made work with the junk we found lying around on the streets and in people's attics. We did a wide variety of soul destroying jobs and ploughed box office receipts into the next piece.

Although things are much better now and as a company we are comparatively well financed, waiting jobs still loom between projects.

List your previous productions?
The first piece was *Perry Como's Christmas Cracker* (1991) which was an insane pantomime nativity play.
Memoirs of an Amnesiac (1992) came to Lancaster and was about a man who builds an museum in his bedsit out of junk and dedicates it to the French composer Erik Satie.
Canute the King (1993) the first version of which was performed in a swimming pool in Birmingham with opera singers and a blues harmonica maestro. The second, only slightly drier version came to the Nuffield.

How do you remember your time at Lancaster in retrospect?
Although I never immersed myself totally in the social side of the University I enjoyed my time there. I was lucky in that the lecturers in Theatre and Independent Studies encouraged me to keep making new work. Many of the mistakes young theatre companies make I was able to make in the secure environment of Lancaster. I was totally obsessed with the subjects and so didn't really notice that work was being done. It certainly didn't feel like three years and I'd gladly do it all again.

Do you feel that being at Lancaster influenced you in any particular way, artistically or otherwise?
When I came to Lancaster I thought theatre was all pantomimes and Shakespeare, so I wanted to make films.

Lancaster disabused me of that idea. The work I saw at the Nuffield Theatre not only changed my idea of what theatre can be but in doing so changed the course of my life, theatre was on the agenda.

Do you think there is a Lancastrian aesthetic or school?
I think you can recognise a thread through the work that has emerged from there. It is something to do with a combination of both a fairly arch theatricality combined with a strong formal concern.

What kind of issues inform your work?
We seem to have developed a group of obsessions surrounding:

- Personal identity and aspiration
- Fate
- The nature of pretending
- Faith in the unlikely

It's about individuals trying to coming to terms with their lives and environment, in many ways it's about us living in Birmingham, which is a curious city in a very curious world. Our sources are very eclectic and there is an implicit political element but it is very subtle, more in the form than the content.

What is your motivation for producing theatre and who are you hoping to reach?
Communication is the main motivation, trying to communicate clearly and directly with people about issues of living today where we do. We hope to reach as many people as possible but we recognise that the form we find the most useful and articulate is not straightforward to some.

Who are you currently receiving funding from?
This is our first project with a full compliment of Arts Council, West Midlands Arts and Birmingham City Council funding. As a result we have been able to make the piece we want to make and pay ourselves a bit. It's luxury.

Will *Bingo in the House of Babel* appeal to any particular sensibility or do you feel that it should have a general appeal?
If you like *Bladerunner*, *Total Recall*, Umberto Ecco, *Heart of Darkness*, have an interest in virtual reality, gratuitous effects, toilet humour or poetry maybe you will like this.

Like I said, you need an open mind but beyond that everyone should get something from it.

April 1995.

The making of *Bingo In The House Of Babel* and the slow remaking of Stan's Cafe

The play *Bingo In The House Of Babel* is about identities in crisis. Looking back on it now, from a distance of twenty six years, it seems clear that it was made by a company whose identity was in crisis.

In 1994 Stan's Cafe was about to make its fourth show in four years and things were changing. Unbeknownst to us we had entered the turbulent passage between promising young company and assured mature company. An Arts Council grant was challenging both our aesthetic and working practices, while personal circumstances were causing us to question who we were.

Leaving the sheltered environment of university to start making shows professionally felt exposing. We were claiming the identity of artists and now had to back that claim up in the arena of public criticism. Having started and named Stan's Cafe, Graeme Rose and I were in the process of shaping the company's characteristics and how it was perceived. It seems logical now that these early shows should be about identity.

Memoirs Of An Amnesiac (1992) staged the interior life of Eric Smith as he struggled to separate himself from his idol, the eccentric French composer Erik Satie. *Canute The King* (1993) found a royal couple wrestling with the tensions between their personal and public identities. *Bingo In The House Of Babel* (1994) could be seen to complete a trilogy, this time with the presence of artificial intelligence calling personal identity into question.

The play's three figures (who could easily be taken as a single character) share the paranoia that they may be robots but don't know how they would know. This idea is inspired by the film *Bladerunner* in which a character is unaware that she is a robot programmed with false memories.

It seemed neat and provocative to place artificially intelligent librarians within an artificial intelligence. This idea was made possible by reading Roger Penrose's book *The Emperor's New Mind* in which he speculates about a vast reference book that could provide answers sufficient to pass the Turing Test for A.I. Presumably such a book would require many volumes, a whole library in fact. A library like this would only be dedicated to an exceptional mind but there may be multiple libraries and they may be stacked on top of each other in a tower.

The idea of a show set in a vast library was made highly attractive by the Jorge Luis Borges short story *The Library Of Babel*, which riffs on the infinite possibilities of such a space. A burnt library felt dramatically powerful, a simple metaphor for a stricken mind and helpfully, saved us having to build a set with thousands of fake book spines in it.

What our set would look like had been a troubling question. Arts Council money meant that we suddenly had a budget line for a set when our aesthetic had been around junk shops and skip diving. We didn't want to change our identity but we did want the Arts Council to see their money put to good use on the stage. To build a substantial set and then set fire to it solved our problem. The set's scale would demonstrate our budget and having it half burnt would stop us looking too slick.

Having a budget also disrupted our working practices. Previously, with no money, we just worked on shows for as long as we wanted. This wasn't difficult as it was mostly just the two of us sharing a house and working whenever we weren't at work. Now, with an Arts Council budget, we were contractually obliged to pay everyone the appropriate mandated wage. We could afford three actors for four weeks. Ironically now that we were 'professional' it felt as if we had less time to make our show - in truth it was probably a similar number of hours more tightly packed - however it worked out it was certainly a big shift in our working culture.

The rehearsal process was a white knuckle ride. Essentially in Week 1 we discussed ideas and tried things out practically through games and improvisation. In Week 2 we tried to keep an experimental 'open to new ideas' approach, but in truth the pressure of opening night was already baring down on us, so we mixed new ideas with developing existing ideas. Week 3 was urgently about developing ideas, structuring and establishing what the show would be like. Week 4 focused on solidifying things, filling in missing bits and polishing what we had. Throughout I was doing bits of writing in the evenings, in response to the day's work, ready for the next day.

I was writing alone, in a rented bedsit, newly and apparently irredeemably single, while around me everyone else seemed to be having fun. For better or worse this show's text became a vent for the darkness of that time.

As a gifted actor Graeme was regularly being offered acting work with other companies that took him out and about, away from Birmingham. In the build up to making *Bingo In The House Of Babel* Graeme was offered a long contract to tour Italy performing in a show with his girlfriend. It was an unbelievable opportunity and he accepted, causing us to ask if Graeme appearing on stage was key to Stan's Cafe's identity.

We agreed in principle that Graeme would contribute to the devising process without being an actor; we did pre-pre-production work together including building the set but in the rehearsal room things were awkward. We had retained Amanda Hadingue from *Canute The King* and recruited Sarah Dawson [now Archdeacon] and Ray Newe through auditions. I remained director but Graeme's role was so unclear that the rehearsal room felt more comfortable when he wasn't there.

Composer Richard Chew seemed to ride the changes more smoothly. Listening back to the soundtrack it is clear that he was trying to push things on from the lush sounds of *Canute The King* and *Memoirs Of An Amnesiac* and the result was a new, thin and more intense sound.

The bigger budget meant we could afford to engage a lighting designer and operator. This was an urgent requirement as in attempting both to direct and operate I would regularly miss cues. My brain would drift from operational thoughts to directorial musings and eventually that musing would involve thinking "we could do with a lighting cue in here" before realising with horror there already was a lighting cue in there and I'd missed it, again! We asked for recommendations and the irrepressible Paul Arvidson was introduced into the expanding Stan's Cafe team.

Bingo In The House Of Babel is an odd show, the figures on stage never really speak to each other. They tend to face front and declaim but it would be a mistake to think that they are speaking to the audience. Perhaps they are all only ever talking to themselves, possibly because all the drama is locked inside their minds, or maybe because they are all robots, programmed to answer questions as librarians and not to interact in other ways with other people.

If, as I contest here, *Bingo In The House Of Babel* was the first show of Stan's Cafe's adolescence, then *Voodoo City* (1995), confrontational, rebellious and painful to make, was the second. After that show there were further convulsions, Graeme left the company for a period and James took up sole artistic directorship*. There was still a lot of growing up to do but perhaps the worst of the gawkiness was over and the company was starting to find its mature identity.

James Yarker, March 2020

*In 1999 Graeme returned to perform in *The Carrier Frequency* and has been a regular with the company ever since.

Ninety Nine Numbers For Finding Lost People

	1 Wishing others choke on their happiness.
	2 Gross Hypocrisy.
Steps to heaven	3 A gut racist fear.
	4 Defaming your best friend.
	5 Arrogance.
	6 Faking liberal attitudes.
	7 Holding knives for far too long.
	8 Thinking of A whilst kissing B.
Vodka & wine	9 Wanting to dive through windows.
Secret den	10 Shitting your pants.
	11 A confession you didn't believe.
	12 Ripping pages from library books.
Unlucky for some	13 Can you remember being one year old?
	14 Never had déjà vu.
	15 Fear of the dark.
	16 Parent's anger.
	17 Protracted fake illness.
	18 Making yourself vomit to avoid weight gain.
Gins in the club house	19 An incident in the bathroom.
	20 Tripping over your own feet.
	21 Fear of juggling.
Two fat blokes	22 Burning toast.

	23 Memory lapses that result in pain.
	24 An inability get out of bed.
Two and One	25 Terrible mental arithmetic.
	26 Forgetting your mother's name.
	27 Falling down stairs.
	28 Tone-deaf singing.
	29 Believing you can change the world.
	30 Cut me, do I not bleed?
Unlucky for some	31 Purple bruising.
	32 Old scars.
	33 Are you colourblind?
	34 Are there numbers printed on your skull?
	35 Ear waggling, can you do it?
	36 Are you left-handed?
	37 Immediate and total intolerance of pain.
	38 Adrenalin rush like hard drugs.
John Buchan	39 Do you suffer hair loss?
	40 Count to a million never losing count.
	41 Wash yourself in noise.
	42 Search for the TV you.
	43 Answer no to every question ever asked.
Severn Bore	44 Drink bleach once in your life.
	45 Tell someone you hate that you love them

Blind	46 Knock yourself unconscious.
	47 Cry your eyes out in a public library.
	48 Burn everything that holds a history.
	49 Hold your breath for ever.
	50 Hiding.
It must be love	51 Thoughts of suicide.
	52 Does Lassie make you cry?
	53 The falling together of galaxies.
	54 Laughter with no obvious cause.
	55 Feeling close when far away.
	56 Prayers for time to break down.
	57 Living a lie for months at a time.
Legs	58 Plain bloody lust.
	59 Testing love through pain.
	60 No, she went of her own accord.
	61 The University of Slough.
Knock Knock	62 Doctor Who?
Miss dialled	63 A directory of hearts never broken.
	64 Black and white and read all over.
	65 Banana skin slipping.
It's brown & sticky	66 A stick.
	67 Put it on my bill.
	68 Take my mother in law, no please take her.

	69 Pure thought is rare.
	70 Never had pins and needles.
	71 Never been the loneliest person in the world.
	72 Always being held.
	73 Never heard English as gibberish.
	74 No knowledge of infinity.
	75 Never woken with a dead arm.
	76 Never had sudden manic strength.
	77 Always know when to stop.
Art is dead	78 Never thrown an inspirational game of darts.
	79 Always been the first to finish.
	80 Knowing what the post brings.
	81 Shit hot telepathy.
	82 Avoidance of falling pianos.
Dangerous pubs	83 By their signs ye shall know them.
	84 Duck!
	85 Synchronicity.
	86 Avoiding walking under ladders.
	87 More than vague interest in astrology.
	88 Knowing lies when you hear them.
	89 Sensing the presence of others.
In the end	90 Have you ever done the impossible?

These bingo calls were used during the randomised section of *Bingo In The House Of Babel*. Despite its title, this list only has ninety numbers as our bingo game only used ninety numbers.

About the illustration and design

The illustrations for the covers of these books were undertaken by students at Birmingham City University as the final module of their first-year illustration course during the Spring/Summer of 2018. The images were developed through workshops using variations of the theatre-devising methods employed by Stan's Cafe but adapted and applied to the making of visual work. The resulting work was shown in the pop-up exhibition *The Something Of Somebody Something* at Stan's Cafe's venue @AE Harris in May 2018.

The design concept of the books was produced by final year Graphic Design student Aimee Chapman. These were then further developed for print in a collaborative process between Stan's Cafe and the University's Innovation Product Support Service (IPSS) which involved helping the company to select appropriate DTP software, undertaking training and selecting a suitable print on demand service.

Gareth Courage
Lecturer in Illustration
Birmingham City University

www.ingramcontent.com/pod-product-compliance
Lightning Source LLC
Chambersburg PA
CBHW071759080526
44588CB00013B/2300